EMDR for Babies

A parents' guide for your baby's first year of life

translated by Sophie Paterson

Ayleen Lyschamaya
Spiritual Master of the Final-Enlightenment

(Dr. rer. pol. Ayleen Birgit Scheffler-Hadenfeldt
Non-medical practitioner in psychotherapy)

Disclaimer: This book has been carefully researched and prepared. Nonetheless, no responsibility shall be taken for the correctness of the content; all information is subject to change. The Author takes no responsibility for any potential damage or consequences arising from the content.

Bibliographic Information from Der Deutschen Bibliothek: The German National Library catalogues this publication in the German National Bibliography; detailed information can be found at http://dnb.ddb.de.

ISBN 978-3-7386-2611-7

Other English parents´ guides of Ayleen Lyschamaya:
Competition-free Birthday: Teamwork Games for Kids: Non-competitive Children's Party Games

1st edition 2015 under Dr. Ayleen Birgit Scheffler-Hadenfeldt
2nd edition 2019 as new publication under Ayleen Lyschamaya
© Ayleen Lyschamaya (Dr. Ayleen Birgit Scheffler-Hadenfeldt)

Manufacture and publishing: BoD – Books on Demand, Norderstedt.

All rights reserved, in whole or in part, including the reprinting of extracts, photomechanical reproduction, use of images, and translation.

Cover image and photos: Relevant global licences exist for professional photos. Any other images have been used with the kind consent and permission of parents or guardians.

Life assumes meaning solely through love.
                                    Hermann Hesse

Contents

	Page
Acknowledgements	6
Foreword	7
What is EMDR?	8
Effects of EMDR	10
How to perform EMDR	14
EMDR techniques	16
Tactile EMDR	17
Auditory EMDR	25
Visual EMDR	30
Video on EMDR techniques	
http://youtu.be/jFIwP4QJbKc	
Full procedure: EMDR for babies	35
Summary: EMDR for babies	36
Processing a birth trauma	37
Resolving trauma for your baby	38
Resolving trauma for you as the mother	43
Summary: resolving a birth trauma	45

Contents

<u>Page</u>

Calming screaming babies — 47
    EMDR for screaming babies — 48
    EMDR as a sleep aid for screaming babies — 50
    EMDR to calm screaming babies — 53
    Looking after yourself — 54
    Summary: calming screaming babies — 58

Preventing ADHD/ADD — 59
    EMDR effect on ADHD/ADD — 59
    Applying EMDR for ADHD/ADD — 63
    Summary: preventing ADHD/ADD — 65

Developing perception skills — 66
    Developing tactile perception — 66
    Developing auditory perception — 67
    Developing visual perception — 68

Limits of self-application — 72
    Limits of EMDR for your baby — 72
    Limits of EMDR for you — 74

Bibliography — 78

About the author — 80

Acknowledgements

I would dearly like to thank my partner Sören Lilienthal and my friend Ines Eckthaler for proofreading this guide and providing further suggestions.

Berlin, June 2019
Ayleen Lyschamaya

A flower needs sun to become a flower.
A human being needs love to become a human being.
Phil Bosmans

Foreword

Dear parents,
EMDR (Eye Movement Desensitization and Reprocessing) is a method used to process emotions and memories, with which you can resolve early childhood issues and optimally encourage your baby's healthy development.

EMDR is an effective and simple technique that is easy to learn and has a completely natural effect. The positive effects of EMDR are based on stimulating both halves of your baby's brain, through touch, hearing and sight.

By using EMDR it is possible to release and resolve emotional blockages, creating a sense of mental and physical relaxation. You have the opportunity to free your baby permanently from distressing feelings, and thus support his or her wellbeing.

Give your baby a good start in life with EMDR and enjoy a wonderful time together. I wish you all the very best.

Yours, Ayleen Lyschamaya

What is EMDR?

EMDR (**E**ye **M**ovement **D**esensitization and **R**eprocessing) was originally a particularly effective psychotherapeutic technique used to process traumatic experiences by means of bilateral stimulation. Bilateral stimulation simply means alternately stimulating the left and right halves of the brain.

Francine Shapiro discovered this method by accident on a stroll in the park. Upon moving her eyes back and forth, she noticed clear relief in her anxiety and depressive thoughts. EMDR has now been internationally recognised as a scientific method in the treatment of post-traumatic stress disorders in adults. [1]

Today, however, different applications of EMDR have been tested, for example to treat anxiety disorders, or relapses in chronic alcoholics. [2]

Since the end of the 1990s, the EMDR method originally developed for adults has also been expanded to treat children: there are studies that are very promising in this area. [3] Initial experiences in the treatment of bonding problems caused by traumata

What is EMDR?

(early mother-child bonding difficulties) have also been positive, which speaks for the successful use of EMDR in this field too. [4]

In summary, EMDR is still a fairly new treatment method, but so successful that it is very quickly spreading and finding use in an increasing number of fields. This guide is intended to demonstrate how you personally can use it to encourage your baby's development.

As a non-medical psychotherapy practitioner, I have plenty of experience with EMDR both personally and in years of application among my clients. I have further developed the original EMDR technique by Francine Shapiro for you and your baby. This parental guide is therefore a very valuable and easy-to-use aid for assisting your baby through his or her first year of life.

Effects of EMDR

EMDR is such an effective method that it can support your baby's development in many respects equally. For example, EMDR can help to resolve common problems in the first year of your child's life and also systematically enables you to develop his or her perception skills.

Birth is the first great stress experienced by your baby, and not every baby processes this well. As a recognised method of trauma therapy, this modified version of EMDR helps to resolve any existing birth-related trauma straight after the event. One possible explanation for its effectiveness is that it mimics REM sleep (Rapid Eye Movement) in its eye movements.

REM sleep is a phase characterised by rapid eye movements, hence the name. Most dreams take place in this particular phase. Babies start to dream even before birth, in their mother's womb. Later, they dream for about 50% of their time asleep, whilst adults only dream for about 20%. Although the precise mechanism of EMDR is still unknown, it is thought that EMDR aids the processing of traumata (e.g. the trauma of birth) in a similar way to our dream mode.

Effects of EMDR

Furthermore, it is supposed that REM sleep represents internal stimulation, which encourages mental development. In this respect, it is likely that EMDR also encourages mental development.

Screaming babies can move parents to despair and cause sleepless nights – and who is then able to maintain a process of continuous loving bonding i.e. a loving parent-child relationship?

When apparently nothing seems to help, EMDR provides a simple method to calm your baby by releasing stressful feelings and generating deep relaxation. Freed from the endless screaming and tension, your love for your baby can then flow freely again and heal the disrupted bonding process, that is to say the strained parent-child relationship. One possible explanation for the liberating effect of EMDR comes from NLP (Neuro-Linguistic Programming).

NLP alters processes in the brain with the aid of language. It is a collection of communication techniques and methods used to modify mental processes. It is known that certain eye movement patterns appear when we cogitate and recall memories, which may possibly explain the liberating and processing effect of EMDR.

Many parents today are afraid of the common diagnosis of Attention Deficit Disorder, with or without the Hyperactivity element (ADHD/ADD). ADHD (Attention Deficit Hyperactivity Disorder) is a behavioural disorder that encompasses inattentiveness, impulsive behaviour and hyperactivity, whilst ADD (Attention Deficit Disorder) involves inattentiveness and impulsive behaviour *without* hyperactivity. To that effect, initial observations give hope that EMDR for babies may be a way of preventing ADHD or ADD in later years.

It is thought that both halves of the brain are synchronised through EMDR's method of bilateral stimulation i.e. both halves clock in at the same speed, so to speak. EMDR encourages the exchange of information between the two halves, which can prevent developmental disorders.

However, independently of scientific research into the positive effects of EMDR (which to date only exists in sufficient amounts concerning adults), from experience EMDR is a natural method that works via

Effects of EMDR

sight, hearing and touch. Astoundingly simple yet target-oriented, EMDR helps to stimulate your baby and thus encourages development.

So help your baby achieve a better quality of life with EMDR – both for now and for later life. Stress that has already been resolved or released in babyhood can open the gates to free-flowing happiness later in life.

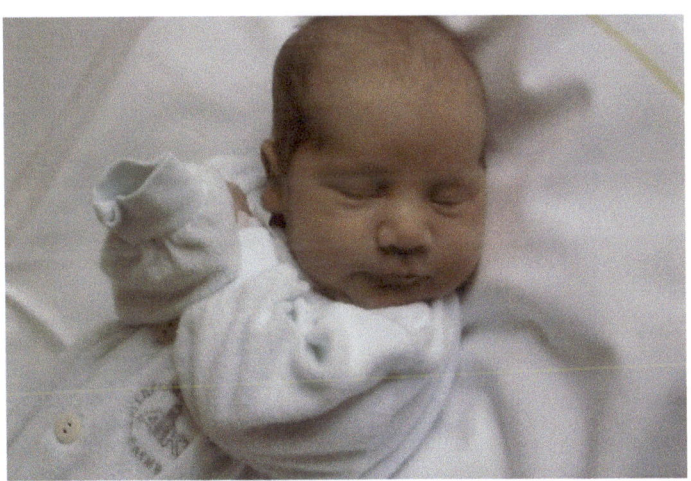

How to perform EMDR

The EMDR method is based on the bilateral i.e. alternate stimulation of both halves of the brain. This can take place via sight, hearing or touch. In psychotherapeutic practice for adults, bilateral stimulation is primarily carried out via the eyes, hence the technique's name "Eye Movement Desensitization and Reprocessing".

Babies, however, must first conquer the world physically – they must 'grasp' things in the truest sense of the word. The tactile EMDR method is therefore the most important for them, which is why I will describe it first.

Thereafter I will introduce the auditory EMDR method and finally the visual EMDR method. Please regard tactile EMDR as the basis onto which auditory and visual EMDR are added (each with somewhat different focal areas). Please use all three EMDR techniques in such a way that will best suit you and your baby.

How to perform EMDR

I recommend using EMDR one to three times a day for around five to ten minutes each time. Always be guided by your baby's wellbeing as well as your own.

Your baby is so sensitive that s/he will perceive whether or not you wish to engage with him/her at that time. By letting your love flow alongside the EMDR techniques, you will encourage development of your baby's most basic sense of trust. However, if you should privately feel – for whatever reason – that carrying out EMDR is an obligation or duty, it is best to leave EMDR for a better time.

Use the EMDR exercises primarily as a way to share time lovingly with your baby, and in doing so naturally encourage his/her development – using bilateral stimulation along the way. The most important thing of all to your baby is your loving attention.

Love each other dearly always.
There is scarcely anything else in the world but that:
to love one another.

Victor Hugo

EMDR techniques

Below I shall introduce the three EMDR techniques: touch, hearing and sight. Tactile EMDR works through brief touches known as 'tapping'. Tapping (= bilateral tapping) means briefly touching your baby's left side and right side alternately using your right and left hand alternately. Tactile EMDR is described in the first section.

In the second section, you will learn more about auditory EMDR (EMDR via hearing). Auditory EMDR takes place via the perception of sound. Finally, in the third section, I will introduce visual EMDR, which takes effect via the eyes.

You can also view the three EMDR techniques at http://youtu.be/jFIwP4QJbKc in which I demonstrate the aforementioned techniques with a doll. Finally, you will also receive an overview of the entire process.

Tactile EMDR

Firstly, I would like to talk a little more about physicality, so that you can better appreciate the great significance of tactile EMDR for your baby.

The body is not only particularly important as a baby; it also has special meaning later as a child and then as an adult. It is the visible reflection of mental processes.

Most people understand this correlation or relationship mainly in terms of psychosomatic illnesses. A close link between body and mind is also demonstrated with the Placebo effect – when someone is given medication that contains no active ingredients and yet the anticipated physical healing takes place regardless, because the person believes in its effect.

In psychotherapy, old emotions and memories stored in the body can be recalled through special exercises. Vice versa, physical limitations or disassociation may be transferred into the psychological or mental state.

Childhood health as well as developmental disorders regularly manifest themselves in the body accordingly. However, not all distinctive features are noticed in preventative medical check-ups.

Gross motor skills, fine motor skills, general coordination and development are mostly well known and are also particularly noticeable in disrupted form as the case may be. Aberrations in these fields are usually easily recognised by paediatricians and parents.

But what about deep sensibility or surface sensibility? If a child, in comparison to other children of his/her age, is noticeably sensitive or insensitive to pain, particularly rough and excessively reckless, then careful attention should be paid, and, if necessary, deep and surface sensibilities should be stimulated.

Does the child use both halves of his/her body in a largely balanced way or does s/he favour one side in particular? Most people have a preferred side, but if a child is clearly unequal, again this should be monitored and the weak side should be nurtured.

How is the child's coordination of upper and lower body? For example, does s/he learn to swing just as well as his or her peers or is s/he apparently lazy and has to be pushed for far longer than the other children?

What about a child's muscle tone? Is it particularly low or particularly high? Is the child's back musculature strong with weak stomach muscles, or vice versa?

Physiotherapeutic help can have a great effect on physical characteristics, even the psyche, and should therefore be taken into account sooner rather than later in the case of conspicuous abnormalities.

If you pay close attention, some of these elements can even be identified in babies. However, noticing abnormalities in your baby is no reason to panic. Each baby develops differently, the range of what is normal is very broad, and in time most will grow out of it.

EMDR creates a solid basis for using both sides of the body equally, right from the outset. Below, I have expanded the usual right-left tapping direction of EMDR to include diagonal movements, in order to encourage coordination between the upper and lower body.

In this respect, you will stimulate healthy mental development in your baby by using physical EMDR. As your baby grows older, you should give him/her plenty of opportunities to experience and try things out physically. You can, for example, use playing and games to effect a positive influence on physical abnormalities, which can then be resolved early on if need be.

The earlier you begin supporting your child's healthy physical and mental development, the less need there will be to catch up and correct it at a later date. As a result, it is beneficial to start EMDR for babies very early on. EMDR for babies can encourage healthy development from the beginning, and thus ease or prevent developmental disorders.

The physical EMDR technique (tactile) is very simple. Bilateral stimulation takes place via touch. After resolving a possible birth trauma (see next chapter), the general approach for tactile EMDR is as follows:

Lay your baby comfortably on his/her back in front of you. This can be in a cot or buggy, on the changing mat or your lap. The important thing is to create a pleasant place for you both, at a nice temperature, where you feel relaxed and well. If you like, you can also carry out the process on soft pillows or cuddled up next to your partner, for example.

Only when both of you – you and your baby – are feeling good, and you yourself are willing to engage with your baby, will you also encourage bonding (early child-parent relationship) through the EMDR – so important for its development.

So make sure contact with your baby is positive: laugh and joke with him/her, whilst continuing to tap his little feet alternately with your palms. Incidentally, you will also be performing EMDR for yourself quite automatically.

   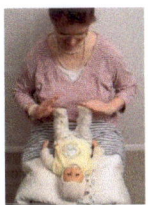
... tap left   tap right   tap left   tap right ...
Bilateral tapping of the feet; http://youtu.be/jFIwP4QJbKc

It is best if your baby's feet are bare, but it is also fine with a romper suit or socks. Simply adapt the strength of the bilateral stimulation correspondingly.

The tapping speed should lie approximately between how someone would tap their foot and yet still be able to coordinate your hands in a relaxed way. However, there is no set precise speed, because everybody is different and each person will prefer a slightly different tempo. Vary the speed and observe how your baby reacts. Then tap at the speed that best suits you both.

A particularly effective form of tapping is to harness the positive effects of the feet's reflexology and acupressure zones. Foot reflexology zones/acupressure (= reflexology) is an alternative treatment based on the idea that all organs and muscle groups are mirrored on the skin of the soles.

In order to harness reflexology/acupressure zones, all you need to do is occasionally use your fingertips instead of your palms for bilateral tapping, and gradually move from your baby's heels to the tip of his toes and back to the heels.

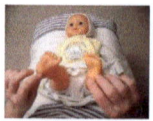 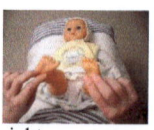  

… bottom left   right   left   top right …
Bilateral reflexology; http://youtu.be/jFIwP4QJbKc

Tactile EMDR

After you have performed EMDR on the feet for a while (and have also moved your fingertips from heels to toes and back), start tapping your palms alternately in a diagonal direction from your baby's left shoulder to right foot. Then tap alternately for approximately the same amount of time from the right shoulder to the left foot.

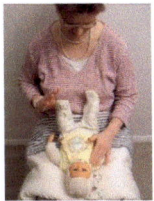   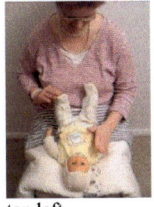

… tap right   tap left   tap right   tap left …
Bilateral tapping on the diagonal; http://youtu.be/jFIwP4QJbKc

Next, touch your baby's left and right shoulder alternately. Smile at your baby and talk lovingly to him/her as you do so: the process should be fun for both of you.

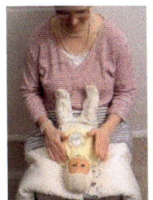 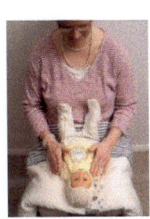 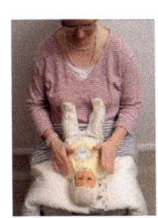 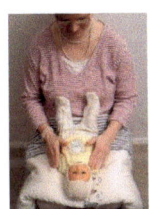

… tap left   tap right   tap left   tap right …
Bilateral tapping of the shoulders; http://youtu.be/jFIwP4QJbKc

Then start tapping in a diagonal direction downwards again. Finally, tap both feet again alternately. Always start and finish with your palms on your baby's feet in order to ground him/her.

After EMDR, give your baby some quiet time to process the session. Tiredness and sleep are typical reactions for all age groups, including adults. Before doing a baby massage, for example, or leaving the house, you should give your baby a break of at least half an hour.

However, please do not forget: the most important thing in the process is the love you convey to your child through words, mimicry and touch.

The mother tongue of love is tenderness.
Ernst Ferstl

Auditory EMDR

Firstly, I would like to introduce you to auditory EMDR therapy, the way I use it with adults and children.

On the market there are special pieces of music that are composed specifically for auditory EMDR therapy. These are available with or without lyrics; from more or less melodious to monotone. However, they all have one thing in common: they always fill the right and left ear with sound in quick alternation. Bilateral stimulation takes place through hearing via headphones.

In therapy, auditory EMDR – unjustly, in my opinion – is not yet as widespread as visual EMDR. The two forms of EMDR supplement each other excellently with their different focal areas.

Adults whose personality system is ruled more by the head, to the point of being detached from their feelings, tend to respond more strongly to auditory EMDR, whilst emotional people respond better to visual EMDR. Both forms of EMDR are therefore each embedded in an overall course of therapy that varies in each case.

Within the framework of holistic spiritual development, I also apply different combinations of both auditory and visual EMDR with tapping foot movements, specifically in order to achieve different subtle layers of awareness.

With children, I use predominantly auditory EMDR to treat ADHD/ADD and developmental disorders, if conventional children's therapies are of no further use. The approach is thus determined by each individual case. Initial experiences with auditory EMDR on children are very promising.

That said, I would like to advise against self-application with bilateral stimulation prompted by EMDR music, because the therapeutic effect can be considerable: application should be in the presence of an expert. As yet there have not been sufficient experiences with EMDR music; it may possibly prompt neurobiological changes.

For babies, regular and direct exposure to EMDR sound via headphones would be too great an intervention in early child development. It should therefore only be used by a therapist specifically to process a trauma in individual cases. Furthermore,

Auditory EMDR

there may be the risk of using EMDR too loudly and for too long if you don't stay with your baby and observe him/her continually.

Instead, the approach is to use totally natural bilateral knocking. The bilateral knocking described below is akin to the drumming used since time immemorial.

Once again, choose a comfortable place for you and your baby. Find somewhere that *you* feel well and happy too. For example, look out for warm light and cheerful colours in your field of vision. Your subconscious will perceive this, and you will be able to relax better to enjoy the time shared with your baby.

For EMDR via hearing, you now need two smaller, solid items for a base (for example two books) and two light drumsticks (for example two pencils). You can also use your hands in place of the drumsticks: simply try out what you prefer. Place the books next to your baby's ears and take one drumstick in each hand as needed.

Firstly, once again touch your baby lovingly; joke and laugh with him/her. Then start drumming on each

Auditory EMDR

base – keep alternating right and left with the drumsticks (or your hands) at a pleasant volume. Whilst doing so, keep the drumstick loose so that you can achieve a high, even speed.

… drum left   drum right   drum left   drum right …
Auditory EMDR; http://youtu.be/jFIwP4QJbKc

Don't underestimate the possible effect on your own self, as you will also be performing EMDR on yourself. This exercise may summon old repressed feelings, which you may then project onto the exercise. If, for example, old wounds of anger are inside you, you may become angry about your own inability to drum well or get annoyed over the exercise itself.

In this case, treat yourself with care and only do as much as is good for you as well. You too have an inner child inside you, which would like to be comforted in its fear and sadness, and must be able to let out its anger harmlessly. So don't get annoyed with yourself; react outwardly to a pillow, or by cleaning your home.

Auditory EMDR

If you would like to combine tactile and auditory EMDR, then start by tapping your baby's feet, continue in both diagonal foot-shoulder directions, and proceed up to the shoulders alone. At this point, move on to the head with auditory EMDR. Then go back to tapping the shoulders, followed by the diagonal shoulder-foot movements, until you are finally back at the feet alone.

Please consider giving your baby a little break of at least half an hour to process the session before stimulating him/her again.

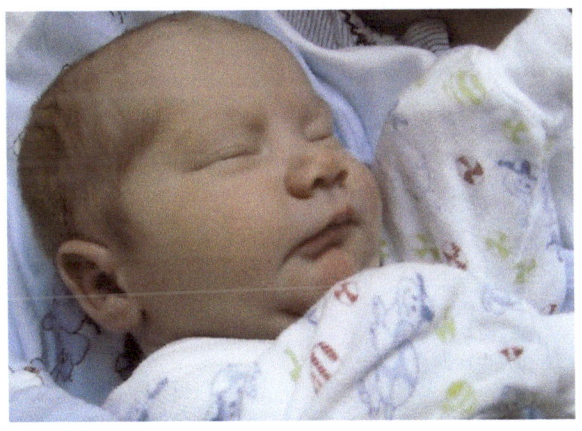

A child is a love made visible.
Novalis

Visual EMDR

EMDR, which stands for "**E**ye **M**ovement **D**esensitization and **R**eprocessing", quite clearly indicates its meaning.

In fact, eye movements are known to happen in dream-processing during REM sleep (Rapid Eye Movement), and from the field of NLP (Neuro-Linguistic Programming) when thinking and recalling memories. In this respect, it is no surprise that the EMDR method is so successful in overcoming traumatic experiences, which depends on the memory and processing of the incident.

Originally used on adults, EMDR has now also become a treatment method for traumatised children and adolescents. EMDR trauma therapy is modified for this younger age group and carried out in eight phases. In individual cases, traumatised infants have also been treated successfully with EMDR.[5]

With traumatised infants, tactile bilateral stimulation is paramount; if need be, it can be supplemented by auditory EMDR. Thus it is the therapeutic work with the attachment figures (psychological parents), not the infant, that takes centre stage.[6]

This parental guide, however, is not about processing trauma therapeutically (excepting birth, which is experienced by everyone), but about the natural encouragement of your baby's development. Through bilateral stimulation, you create stimuli that your baby will follow with his/her eyes for as long as s/he can and is beneficial.

EMDR via sight is a valuable stimulation for your baby, because some developmental disorders and indeed particularly traumatic experiences manifest themselves in the inability of the eyes to follow your finger or an object fluidly; instead jumping in fits and starts.

But don't worry – you will not be able to recognise a developmental disorder through eye movement in babyhood, because your baby will simply be distracted: there are more interesting things to see than an object or finger just disappearing from view. Despite this, use this approach to practise fluid eye movements in play and thus encourage healthy development.

Visual EMDR

Naturally, babies are most interested in faces, so visual bilateral stimulation may only work briefly or even not at all. Don't be disappointed: be relaxed and simply test it out repeatedly in play. Babies still have to learn every kind of coordination to an adequate extent, so it is enough if you establish positive development stimuli in play.

It is helpful to use something interesting for visual bilateral stimulation, for example something glittery. Shiny birthday straws or flashing pens are particularly suitable. And then off you go.

Seek out a comfortable position in a pleasant spot for you and your baby. Use this shared time together to make yourself feel good. For example, drink a delicious tea in your favourite flavour and listen to some nice music.

With visual EMDR, this time you can also hold your baby in your arm, as you only need one hand to perform visual EMDR. Use your free hand to hold a small, interesting object or stretch out your index finger and wave it repeatedly from left to right in front of your baby's eyes. Your baby's little head shouldn't move along with it; only his/her eyes should follow your finger or object.

... fluid   movement   from one side   to the other ...

Visual EMDR; http://youtu.be/jFIwP4QJbKc

Your finger or object should be around fifteen centimetres from your baby's eyes. The speed of your finger or object is guided by how fast your baby can follow it with his/her eyes. So move your finger or object from right to left, as far as your baby's eyes can

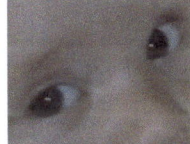

follow it right up to the corner of his/her eye. Your baby's head should remain still, so that only the eyes move.

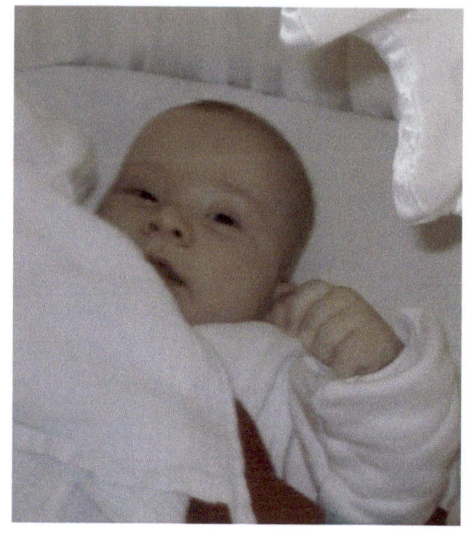

A single look of love
gives strength to the soul.
Jeremias Gotthelf

Full procedure: EMDR for babies

If you would like to combine tactile, auditory and visual EMDR with each other, start by tapping your baby's feet, then tap diagonally from shoulder to foot in both directions, and finally tap the shoulders. Then move on to auditory EMDR, making sounds rapidly and bilaterally next to the ears. This is followed by visual EMDR: moving your finger or object back and forth in front of your baby's eyes. Finally, tap the shoulders, tap diagonally from shoulder to foot, and tap the feet again.

Please give your baby a rest after EMDR for the purpose of inner processing. This should last at least half an hour.

And of course: remember that love for your baby is more important than all the techniques. If you feel the impulse to tenderly cuddle and cradle your baby, please do so. Then you can continue with EMDR.

Summary: EMDR for babies

Aim: encourage development, develop perception skills, process stress, improve bonding.

Application: 1-3 times per day.

Duration: 5-10 minutes.

Approach: tactile, auditory, visual, tactile EMDR.

Tactile EMDR
Tapping the feet with palms,
(Tapping the feet as reflexology/acupressure zones),
Tapping diagonally: right foot /left shoulder,
Tapping diagonally: left foot/right shoulder,
Tapping the shoulders.

Auditory EMDR
Bilateral drumming next to the ears.

Visual EMDR
Bilateral movements in front of the eyes.

Tactile EMDR
Tapping the shoulders,
Tapping the diagonals,
Tapping the feet.

Rest phase: at least ½ hour break.

Processing a birth trauma

You as a mother should perform the EMDR to work through the experience of birth, because it was you that shared this deeply moving, unique experience with your baby. A significant other may take on this task only if you yourself are unable to do so for whatever reason.

You probably experienced natural birth as an intensive shared liminal experience. Perhaps it was a deeply moving, positive experience for you; perhaps negative sensations overwhelmed you. Yet even if aid was administered during the birth or a caesarean was necessary, the moment you held your baby in your arms for the first time is always unique. My aim is therefore firstly to provide support for working through a trauma experienced by your baby, but also to approach you personally as a mother.

To conclude this section is a summary of the EMDR process for resolving a traumatic birth experienced by your baby.

Resolving trauma for your baby

It has recently been ascertained through research into infants that each individual experiences much more before and during birth than was previously thought.[7] First and foremost, birth is a totally natural process. It only becomes a trauma if your baby's ability or opportunity to adjust and cope are overstretched.

Normally, after the birth, babies are able to process mild to moderate trauma themselves.[8] However, you can ease this natural processing by supporting your baby with EMDR. It is very important to work through the birth well, because this can have an impact on the rest of your child's life.

Birth experiences are imprinted as basic patterns and are recalled when problems occur in later life. In particular, difficult transition situations can activate the long-embedded patterns of resolution.[9] In this respect, it is important for your baby to process his or her birth as well as possible in order to be able to better cope with difficult situations in later life.

Among adults, therapy is sometimes used to resolve a traumatic birth through hypnosis or physical therapy reliving the incident, if the birth pattern is having an impact on the life of the person concerned. By using

Processing a birth trauma

early EMDR processing, you can prevent this in your baby from the outset.

As the birth experience is later remembered predominantly physically in similar situations,[10] tactile EMDR with tapping is the preferred method for resolving a birth trauma. Added to this is visual EMDR, because the eyes are particularly important when it comes to processing trauma.

When carrying out EMDR with your baby for the first time, or the first two or three times, it is quite likely that your baby will process his or her birth and possible birth trauma. This can temporarily lead to what is known as "abreacting" (a kind of catharsis), as the stressful feelings drain away. Abreacting means that your baby may start to grizzle, cry or even scream; intensified breathing or spitting is also possible.

This discomfort is nothing more than the release of energy bound to the birth trauma: the birth trauma thus loses its emotional charge. Just remember that you are doing no more than touching your baby and waving a finger or interesting object in front of his/her eyes – these unpleasant feelings therefore cannot be caused by you at all; rather, they must already have been stored in your baby.

Processing a birth trauma

In order to release the trauma of birth completely, everything that was stored in your baby must flow out. For this reason, continue tapping not only for five to ten minutes, but until your baby abreacts; that is to say has calmed down again. The complete EMDR process therefore runs from your baby's neutral original state to an emotional abreaction to peace and contentment; at this point your baby will probably fall asleep.

It is important that you do not let yourself become distressed, in case your baby begins to feel ill at ease. Those disquieting memories can flow out with greater ease the more your baby feels protected in your reassuring care.

Releasing a birth trauma is a very demanding process for your baby. If you ascertain that your baby obviously had a lot to process during your first EMDR session (a longer emotional process has taken place), you should wait around three days before carrying out EMDR again. Over this time, it may well be that the process is continuing by itself – so perhaps your baby is a little more fretful than otherwise. In this case, simply comfort him/her lovingly, as it is an expression of his inner healing process.

Only if your baby continues to react uncomfortably to EMDR after about three full EMDR sessions (in each case up to the calming point) and an interval of about three days each time, should you clarify the causes before continuing with EMDR. Please consider the chapter on ADHD/ADD and the limits of self-application of EMDR.

Sometimes it may be that your baby doesn't abreact to the full degree, but instead repeatedly feels rather ill at ease during short daily sessions. This is a weaker abreaction process distributed over a longer period, and is completely normal. After an initial boost, a state of contentment would finally have to be reached, when the unpleasant feelings have drained away.

For the first few applications of EMDR, you should have plenty of time available, because you don't know how your baby will react. The important thing, however, is to continue tapping until the traumatic feelings have drained away enough for your baby to calm down. So please plan generous time for your baby.

When carrying out EMDR to release a birth trauma, the process mimics the process of birth and the baby's physical arrival on earth by moving from the head to the feet. This makes sense particularly for caesarean section babies, whose abrupt passage into life is

Processing a birth trauma

gradually smoothed and thus earthed and stabilised by means of this process.

Start by tapping the head carefully to release the birth trauma. Even if your baby's head endured a lot during birth, here it is only a matter of a light stimulating touch above the ears. After a while, start applying visual EMDR for as long as your baby follows your finger or object with his/her eyes. Then move on to tapping the shoulders, and finally (without tapping the shoulder/foot diagonals) go directly to the feet.

Tap the shoulders for longer than the head, and the feet longest in order to ground your infant well. If necessary, tap the feet until the emotional abreaction process is over.

If you don't know whether birth may have been traumatic for your baby, use this method of tapping for one to three times and then move on to the full EMDR approach. For caesarean sections, you should perform the 'birth trauma tapping' for about three to five times in order to ground your baby more smoothly before moving on to the general process of EMDR for babies.

Resolving trauma for you as the mother

As mother, you are the most important person to your baby. But you can only take loving care of him/her if you have the strength. This is why I kindly urge you to look after yourself well too.

If the birth was traumatic for you, you should not live with this strain permanently. Do something positive for yourself and ask for professional support. It is quite possible to process the birth trauma at once using EMDR specifically for adults, if you have stored only this experience as a trauma. Make the most of the opportunity to free yourself permanently from unpleasant feelings.

If you are not only struggling with the trauma of your baby's birth but also aware of old traumata from your childhood, or cannot accept or allow feelings as someone who lives by their head, it is best not to carry out EMDR for birth trauma on your baby yourself. Leave the bilateral stimulation to another caring significant other. Indeed, you may find that tapping your baby over a lengthier period also releases abreactions in yourself.

However, if you are able to let your feelings flow out, if need be, you can carry out the tapping on your baby yourself, even if you have not quite processed the

Processing a birth trauma

birth experience completely. You will then process it together with your baby, as the case may be.

When performing EMDR on your child, do not be afraid that showing your feelings could harm your baby – quite the contrary. Your baby had already been secure in your tummy with your feelings for nine months. Yet in general too, small children cope very well with genuinely perceived feelings in other people, because they themselves are still so intensively connected to their own.

If you feel like crying or experience fear, let your tears fall and protect and shelter your inner child too. If you feel anger, do not direct anger towards your baby or yourself in your thoughts, but simply let it flow out as energy. You can also tread or stamp your feet on the floor to the rhythm of the tapping.

In order to comfort your own inner child, and make him feel protected and safe, music can be very helpful. You and your baby can listen to comforting lullabies when you are tapping, if this does you good. There is a CD by *Shaina Noll, Songs for the Inner Child*, which supports the outflow of emotion.

However, whether with or without music, allow yourself to experience your feelings, so that they can flow out. Be as loving with yourself as with your baby, as it is also a healing process for you. Together, you and your baby can free yourself from burdensome feelings through EMDR.

Summary: resolving a birth trauma

Aim: to resolve/release birth trauma.

Application: 1-5 times at an interval of 3 days each time.

Duration: 15-20 minutes
or longer until calm replaces abreaction.

Approach: tactile, visual, tactile EMDR.

Tactile EMDR
Tapping the head for about 3 minutes,

Visual EMDR

Tactile EMDR
Tapping the shoulders for about 5 minutes,
Tapping the feet for about 7 minutes,
or until there is calm.

Rest phase: at least 1 hour rest.

Processing a birth trauma

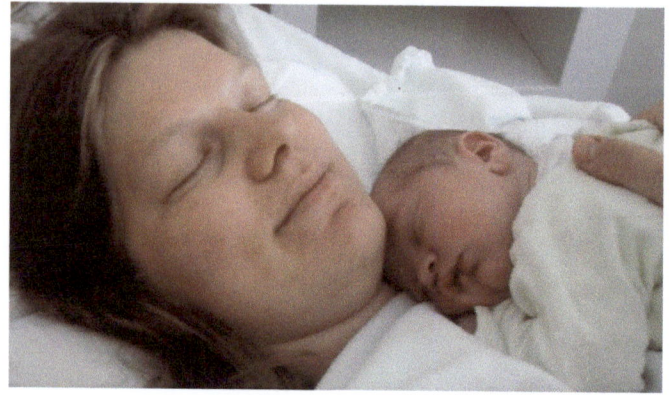

*A mother is the only person in the world
who already loves you before she knows you.*
Heinrich Pestalozzi

Calming screaming babies

If you have a constantly screaming baby (apparently for no reason), you will find yourself in a particularly demanding situation that can lead to despair. Above all, one's own helplessness can hardly be endured.

Yet with EMDR, you are no longer a slave to the situation. EMDR is a particularly effective therapeutic method that you can use to help your baby. Ultimately, EMDR is specifically designed to better process emotional strain.

Below, I will introduce EMDR in general for use on screaming babies. After that, you will learn how to carry out EMDR to help your baby fall asleep for a regulated daily routine. I will then outline ways to calm your baby using EMDR at the moment of acute screaming.

I also have a few more suggestions for you as parents, since the younger the children, the more important and greater your influence. Finally, an overview will sum everything up.

EMDR for screaming babies

Screaming is totally normal behaviour in babies – to attract attention to their own wishes and needs. We only talk about excessive screaming when the so-called 'rule of three' has been met: screaming occurs over a period of at least three weeks on at least three days per week for more than three hours per day.

Around 20 per cent of all babies are affected by this. If nothing helps – not feeding, not changing nappies, comforting or carrying about – it can move parents to desperation. It is particularly bad especially in the first three months of life, but afterwards usually gets better.

The causes of excessive screaming in babies is unknown. Physical causes such as respiratory system infections, inflammation of the middle ear and urinary tract infections must first be ruled out. Likewise, stomach-bowel diseases may be responsible, and digestive disorders (the so-called three-month colic) are frequently cited as the cause. Please clarify your baby's health with a paediatrician first.

Other causes are to be found in the social field. The parent-child relationship is very complex and also involves non-verbal communication based on mimicry, sound and touch, as well as elements that are unknown to the parents. Don't be afraid of requesting aid.

Birth traumata too are thought to be a cause for apparently groundless screaming. Excessive crying indicates that your baby is not coping well with processing the trauma on its own. In this case, EMDR is the best aid and you should proceed as described in the previous chapter on birth trauma.

Screaming infants can also have a problem self-regulating. This means that they react more strongly to external stimuli than other babies, and are therefore more easily excitable. Please also read the chapter on ADHD/ADD.

If a lower ability to self-regulate is the cause of excessive screaming, a less stimulating environment, a regulated daily routine and lots of loving physical contact are recommended.

Tactile EMDR automatically gives your baby this physical contact and positive attention. Consequently, you should schedule EMDR into your daily routine, preferably in order to initiate sleeping times.

This means that you need not be afraid of overloading your infant with additional stimuli. Quiet and constantly repeated bilateral stimulation is beneficial for centring the many external stimuli, and encourages your baby to process these and reach a state of calm.

Before starting EMDR on a screaming baby, however, you yourself should take some time out to recover adequately from all the tension, sleepless nights and desperation. This will enable you to carry out EMDR in the first place. As an exhausted mother and tetchy father, allow yourself some help from friends or relatives, so that you can get some rest and attain an inner peace.

When you are ready to have inner contact with your baby again, firstly carry out EMDR to process a possible birth trauma. Then apply EMDR to support your baby's self-regulation.

EMDR as a sleep aid for screaming babies

Firstly, draw up a day plan with regular sleeping times for your baby. During these times, you should reduce the stimuli in your baby's environment as much as possible, and above all make it dark and quiet. If you hold your baby to your body in a sling, you should enjoy a comfortable break (by, for example, reading or listening to music via headphones).

Always start sleeping times in the same way: tap the feet so that your baby gets used to this sleep-time ritual. Keep tapping only the feet until your baby has relaxed enough on the whole to no longer be a screaming baby.

As a sleep-time ritual, EMDR must only be carried out by tapping the feet – this is in order not to interrupt the monotony being established. So to start with, tap at a normal speed for quite a while, then gradually more slowly, in order to guide your baby to sleep. Finally, you can gradually and evenly reduce the speed to about one tap per second.

At each session, tap your baby's feet until s/he has fallen asleep. Over time, the act of falling asleep will speed up thanks to the ritualisation, processing and general increase in relaxation. Once your baby's screaming and sleep behaviour has normalised, you can continue general EMDR as described.

Calming screaming babies

In the beginning, it is nice to talk lovingly to your baby, but gradually you should only look fondly at him or her to encourage peace and finally sleep. Stay with your baby inwardly, as s/he will sense the love or whether you are only "acting mechanically".

Perhaps viewing your child as a miracle of nature will help you to focus positively on him/her. What is happening in this tiny thing, just to survive at all? Look at those cute little fingers that will one day become the adult hand of a man or woman... Fascinating to think how much this tiny helpless being needs you now, and what he or she will later be able to do on his/her own... Enjoy these moments with your baby, as your child will grow up and go his/her own way very fast.

You can also go one step further and try to put yourself in your baby's shoes. What does your baby feel right now? How does s/he see the world? The book by Daniel N. Stern *Diary of a Baby: What Your Child Sees, Feels and Experiences* may help. This perspective develops your empathy and strengthens bonding with your baby.

Lastly, you can also picture a lovely future with your child. What would you like to pass on to him/her?

What great things will you do together? What positive things do you wish for your child?

EMDR to calm screaming babies

If your baby is screaming, of course please check first of all whether there is something s/he needs. Then simply pick up your baby with love. Not every inexplicable bout of screaming needs to be ended immediately.

The value of your parenthood does not depend on how quickly you can calm your baby, but how lovingly you can accept and embrace your screaming infant. So no pressure or hurry: instead, treat your little bawler fondly and affectionately.

Perhaps it helps to imagine what you yourself would want if things were going badly for you. A low-key, loving presence or support conveys comfort and a feeling of security in all discomforts.

Of course, some adults would rather retreat and be alone if things are not going well, but after nine months of the closest proximity in a mother's tummy, your baby has not yet developed this need for distance.

If you would still like to calm your baby with EMDR after this process of loving acceptance, then pick up the appropriate EMDR technique where it is. Therefore start with auditory EMDR.

With auditory EMDR, you don't need to drown your baby's noise level, as even the fluctuations have a very subtle effect. Perform auditory EMDR consistently for a while, and look fondly at your baby.

Don't forget that your baby is not screaming to annoy you, but because s/he doesn't feel well for whatever reason. But you are not responsible for his/her ill-being when you have done everything you can to help. Stay with him/her inwardly, and perform the bilateral stimulation on your child kindly and in a warm manner.

After a while of carrying out auditory EMDR, move on to tapping the feet. Tap in the sleep-aid method described above, gradually slowing your movements until your baby has become calm.

Looking after yourself

Staying relaxed when your baby is constantly screaming, and cannot be calmed by anything, is such

Calming screaming babies

an enormous challenge that you should not be afraid of accepting every possible assistance. Unfortunately, your own tension will lead to your baby screaming even more. Before you know it, you are in a vicious circle of increasing strain.

EMDR can calm your baby, but at the same time you should also be kind to yourself. Organise enough time out that will help you find peace.

In addition, you can combine EMDR on your baby with the following exercise on yourself (to relieve stress):

Breathe calmly, deeply and evenly through the nose and exhale audibly through the mouth. Your breathing rhythm can be adapted to your tapping, but is not absolutely necessary.

When breathing in through the nose, imagine strength flowing into your body through the soles of your feet and spreading through it. When exhaling through the mouth, picture all your stresses and strains flowing out of your body, like in a shower.

Calming screaming babies

Don't worry if you can't quite picture this fully: your subconscious will respond to the attempt, and your power of imagination will get better and better over time.

Likewise, there is no need to worry that you are no longer inwardly attuned to your baby enough. When you are inwardly attuned to yourself, you are much more deeply connected to your baby than you could ever be through everyday contact.

So look after yourself well, as only then will you have the necessary strength to take care of your baby well. And only then will you yourself be balanced enough to be connected to your baby in loving bonding.

Affectionate bonding also includes allowing yourself to be sour with your baby from time to time. After all, you as a parent are only human – and perfect parents do not exist. But you are a good parent anyway, as otherwise you would not be taking the trouble to read this book. So please be kind to yourself.

Perhaps it will help you to think about how short the period of screaming is compared to the life

Calming screaming babies

stretching out before your baby. Looking back, this screaming will only be a memory recounted on odd occasions.

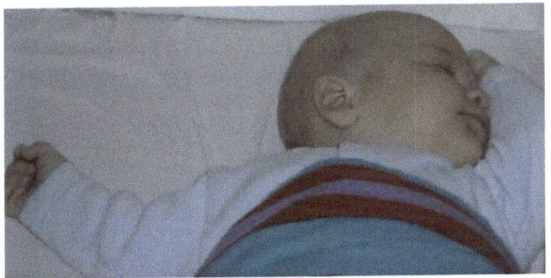

Summary: calming screaming babies

Aim: sleep aid, calming, improve bonding.

Application: sleep-time ritual or for continued crying.

Duration: until your baby falls asleep or is calm.

Approach:

    1) Sleeping aid: tactile EMDR.
    Tapping the feet, becoming slower and slower.

    2) Calming: auditory, tactile EMDR.
    Satisfying needs,
    Picking up your baby lovingly
                    and comforting him/her,
    Auditory EMDR,
    Tapping the feet, becoming slower and slower.

Rest phase: at least ½ hour break.

Love is a decision to say yes to everything about a person, no matter what the particulars.
Otto Flake

Preventing ADHD/ADD

These days, we encounter Attention Deficit Disorder with or without hyperactivity (ADHD/ADD) so often in everyday life – almost always linked to problems – that many parents are afraid of this diagnosis.

EMDR offers the chance to prevent ADHD/ADD, or if need be to exercise a beneficial effect on the course of the disorder. Firstly I will explain how and why EMDR is thought to have a positive effect on ADHD/ADD. You will then learn how to proceed in the case of a possible predisposition towards ADHD/ADD. Finally, once again you will receive an overview of how to apply the EMDR.

EMDR effect on ADHD/ADD

Attention Deficit Disorder (with or without Hyperactivity) involves difficulty filtering stimuli and controlling impulse – intelligence is normal, indeed often above average.

Attention **D**eficit **H**yperactivity **D**isorder (ADHD) is today the most common behavioural disorder among children and young people. Boys are markedly more frequently affected than girls. ADHD symptoms continue into adulthood in about one third of people.[11]

The basic characteristics of ADHD are:
− Disrupted attention; a lack of staying power when undertaking tasks; the tendency to switch activities before they are concluded.
− Restless behaviour, in particular the inability to sit still.
− Impulsiveness with abrupt actions that are not appropriate in the social context.[12]

If hyperactivity is not the focus, as in the German children's story *Fidgety Philip*, but rather difficulty paying attention as in *Johnny Head-in-the-Clouds*, we talk about **A**ttention **D**eficit **D**isorder (ADD). Girls are more commonly affected by ADD than boys. Symptoms common to both ADHD and ADD include impulsive behaviour and a lack of attention, only with ADHD there is added hyperactivity.

These children and their relatives are usually under considerable pressure because failure in school and the development of other emotional disorders are frequent. Therefore, it is advisable to prevent ADHD/ADD as far as possible.

Preventing ADHD/ADD

Of course, it is difficult to prevent ADHD/ADD when the original cause of the disorder is still not clearly known. It is believed to stem from a combination of biological, psychological and social factors. Due to familial clustering (in other words it runs in the family), a hereditary signal deviation in the brain is cited as a main reason.

Medication is therefore frequently administered to improve attention, concentration and self-control, as well as relieve the psychological strain on the child. Stimulants are prescribed primarily for the medical treatment of ADHD/ADD, which influence signal transfer in the brain.

Stimulants boost neural activity in the brain. Stimulating ADHD/ADD medication improves stimuli transfer in the brain and can therefore enhance concentration, staying power and attention. The transfer of information between nerve cells in the brain works better through the medication.

The positive effect of this kind of medication among ADHD/ADD patients suggests that early bilateral stimulation through EMDR may also have a positive effect on the prevention of ADHD/ADD.

Preventing ADHD/ADD

After all, you are setting targeted bilateral impulses that are processed in the brain. EMDR stimulates the transfer of information in your baby's brain in a totally natural way – without medication.

It has also been observed that the sleeping patterns of ADHD children often deviate from those of other children. In particular, the REM-phases seem to be shorter, longer or more frequently interrupted.[13] Accordingly, it makes sense to stimulate the eyes bilaterally to prevent ADHD/ADD, because EMDR is naturally modelled on the eye movements of REM sleep.

If ADHD/ADD is already present in your family, your baby could be genetically predisposed to it. As a result, you should support your baby's brain development in a natural way right from the outset – using EMDR to stimulate the brain's transfer of stimuli without overwhelming it.

My experience with older children is that auditory EMDR with a music CD encourages concentration and attention, but most of all can reduce motor restlessness. Overly intensive application of EMDR may lead to headaches at the start, so please introduce it particularly slowly if ADHD/ADD is suspected.

Applying EMDR for ADHD/ADD

In the case of possible ADHD/ADD, firstly stick with more frequent but very short EMDR sessions lasting five minutes at the most. If there is a history of ADHD/ADD in the family, you should introduce EMDR very slowly over several weeks.

A possible additional birth trauma would therefore only be resolved slowly, but this is better than overstraining your baby. It is highly likely that the abreaction will manifest itself more weakly, but will lead to some discomfort during and after the EMDR over a longer period. This is then a sign of feelings of strain being released over time using EMDR.

For a possible ADHD/ADD baby, carry out the process three to five times per day for the first week (each session lasting five minutes): simply tap the feet before adding the shoulders in the second week, and the more complex diagonal direction in the third. The sequence then remains as previously described: feet, diagonals, shoulders, diagonals, feet (except that you should leave out the diagonals in the second week).

If you have the impression that your baby feels fine receiving tactile EMDR, replace one of the daily EMDR sessions with auditory EMDR. During these five minutes, you will only carry out EMDR through hearing.

If your baby seems fine with this as well, go on to visual bilateral stimulation. Please replace another session of EMDR with EMDR for the eyes. It doesn't have to go "perfectly"; you just need to keep providing your baby with stimuli that promote development.

If your baby is okay with the individual EMDR techniques, you can gradually combine them and slowly increase the length of the EMDR session from five to ten minutes. At this point, step-by-step you will have reached the general EMDR approach described and intended for all babies.

In the case of possible ADHD/ADD, please take care to introduce all other uses and applications of EMDR (such as developing perception skills) more slowly and gradually over a longer period.

Summary: preventing ADHD/ADD

Application: 3-5 times daily.

Duration: 5 minutes.

Approach: EMDR that expands weekly.

Week 1
Tapping the feet 3-5 times per day.

Week 2
Tapping the feet, shoulders, feet 3-5 times per day.

Week 3
Tapping the feet, diagonals, shoulders, diagonals, feet 3-5 times per day.

Week 4
Tapping 2-4 times per day, as in Week 3,
Auditory EMDR 1 x per day.

Week 5
Tapping 1-3 times per day, as in Week 3,
Auditory EMDR 1 x per day,
Visual EMDR 1 x per day.

Week 6
Gradually transition to full process.

Developing perception skills

If you are doing well combining bilateral stimulation with spending loving time with your baby, then you can turn your attention to developing the three different forms of perception: touch, hearing and sight. Continue the basic form of EMDR regularly, and replace it from time to time with the expanded techniques for developing perception skills in play as described below.

Developing tactile perception

Your baby would like to 'grasp' the world in the truest sense of the word: s/he perceives it in a very physical way. As a result, your baby needs body contact in order to develop well. Through body contact, your baby is able to feel his/her own body not to mention personal boundaries.

In some cultures, babies had – and have – constant body contact because they are carried in a sling. So don't worry that you will overwhelm your baby with body contact; quite the opposite.

Convey valuable body experience to your baby through full-body bilateral stimulation. The only point to remember here is to touch each side of your infant's body alternately. Everything else can be left to your creativity.

For example, sometimes you might like to use flat palms, sometimes just your fingertips or sometimes even different objects. Fabric feels different to a feather or a spoon. Sometimes you can exert more pressure; other times not so much. Tapping can take the form of knocking, stroking or tickling. You can also vary the speed of your tapping, or make a surprising stimulus on unexpected parts of the body. Give your imagination free rein!

It is important that you and your baby have fun together. Joke and laugh with him/her, and if you feel the urge to cuddle, then do so. You can continue bilateral stimulation another time.

Developing auditory perception

With this technique via hearing, expanded to involve play, vary the sounds you make next to each of your baby's ears alternately.

Sometimes you can make louder noises, other times quieter; sometimes faster, sometimes slower.

Sometimes you can use your fingers or different objects. You can also move the sources of noise closer to your baby's ears, or further away. Once again, you can let your creativity run wild.

It is particularly nice to sing lullabies whilst simultaneously tapping the rhythm bilaterally. Perhaps you could even hum or whistle a children's song.

Another possibility is to put different styles of music on in the background, whilst you continue the bilateral stimulation and observe how your child reacts to classical music, for example. In this case, do not try to follow the rhythm, but simply tap consistently and evenly.

Once again, it is vitally important that you both have fun in this shared musical journey of discovery.

Developing visual perception

Developing visual perception has its limits in how far your baby follows you with his/her eyes. Let things proceed in a fun way and lower your expectations.

You can vary the bilateral stimulation of the eyes by moving your finger or object at different speeds,

Developing perception skills

sometimes moving it further away and sometimes bringing it close to your baby's eyes.

Various patterns are also possible, which should contain the basic movement from left to right and back again – right to the corner of the eye. Thus for example, you can make zig-zag lines up and down or from left to right. You can also draw diagonal lines in the air.

When drawing circles in both directions, please bear in mind that your baby's eyes follow the circle to the edge. You can also draw figures-of-eight horizontally or vertically in the air. For horizontal figures-of-eight, move your finger or object above the nose and upward and back down to the side.

Babies are fascinated by soap bubbles – but please only use these where possible flecks and splotches won't disturb. If you are holding your baby looking away from you, someone (perhaps a sibling?) can blow soap bubbles while you turn yourself from side to side so that s/he is obliged to move his/her eyes accordingly if it wants to see the soap bubbles. To do so, rest your baby's head against you in such a way that s/he can't move it, but instead has to move his/her eyes.

Developing perception skills

Incidentally, this is a good opportunity to encourage fluid eye movements in ordinary everyday life. If something fascinates your baby, simply take the opportunity to cradle him/her gently in your arm.

It is also possible to combine visual and auditory perception-developing methods. For example, you can clap your hands by your baby's left and right ear alternately, thus moving your hands from one side to the other in front of your baby's eyes.

Give your creativity free rein and have fun with your baby.

Developing perception skills

I come into this world and search for nothing but love.
Author unknown

Limits of self-application

By using touch, hearing and sight, EMDR is a completely natural method: for example, we tap our feet automatically as we walk. Yet EMDR is also a very effective therapeutic technique – a couple of points must therefore be observed before using EMDR on your baby.

Firstly, some information on what to look for with your baby, followed by a couple of tips for yourself.

Limits of EMDR for your baby

Firstly, your baby should have arrived on roughly the expected date. EMDR is not to be used on premature infants, because your baby would not have been directly stimulated in the womb. Indeed, you should not start EMDR even on the actual due date with a premature baby, because your baby's development may have been delayed. So before commencing EMDR with a premature infant, please talk to your attending paediatrician.

Furthermore, your baby should be completely healthy. If s/he has any illnesses or physical impairments, please consult with your practising

Limits of self-application

paediatrician first. Atypical movement patterns must also be clarified with a doctor before applying EMDR. On the other hand, Caesarean, forceps or suction deliveries do not pose an obstacle for carrying out EMDR, provided that your baby is healthy.

Moreover, EMDR must only be used when your baby can enjoy a healthy, stable environment that meets his/her natural requirements. Instead of resolving situational strain, EMDR could actually imprint the strain of an ongoing unsuitable life situation more intensively.

If your baby has lived through a traumatic experience not accordant with his/her age, such as separation from his/her most important attachment figure, medical procedures, accidents or violence, EMDR must be accompanied by competent psychotherapy. You alone are then overtaxed.

The older your child grows, the more s/he gathers experiences to be processed and the less adaptable the psyche becomes. Therefore, as time goes on, you should also be aware of increasingly strong abreactions. As a result, in older children and adults EMDR must always be carried out with therapeutic support (first and foremost with bilateral stimulation of the eyes).

As processing possibilities vary widely (as do individual stresses and strains), there are no universal rules on up to what age you can independently start using EMDR to stimulate development, or until when EMDR must be accompanied by therapy.

As a rule (in the normal case), I can recommend EMDR for developmental support commencing from after birth to twelve months i.e. within your baby's first year – at this age the psyche is still fully open and babies are naturally connected to their inner powers of self-healing.

At this age possible abreactions remain manageable when traumatic experiences are restricted to the birth, as the case may be. You can then continue to use EMDR independently beyond this age for as long as it continues to do your child good. For example, EMDR could be a good bedtime ritual.

Limits of EMDR for you

If it is not possible for you to establish an inner relationship with your baby, you should stop any

Limits of self-application

EMDR and clarify the causes with yourself psychotherapeutically. It could be linked to your own repressed traumata in early life.

For the loving early bond between you and your baby, it is important that you are emotionally able to engage inwardly with your child. But even if you do not immediately succeed, initial promising studies suggest that EMDR heals initial inner separation retroactively and assists the development of healthy bonding.[14]

If you are experiencing any other psychological dysfunction, you should have this treated before using EMDR on your baby. Speak to your therapist as regards how far you are able to carry out this method.

In essence, however, you can use EMDR on your baby if it helps you both to overcome your own traumatic past or emotional disturbance. A decisive factor here is how you cope with a possible EMDR effect on yourself. Please seek advice from a psychotherapist.

EMDR is, however, a natural but also very effective method, which – just like any other – should be applied

Limits of self-application

responsibly. Please consider the information provided here, and seek the advice of experts if necessary. Ultimately, it is you that is responsible for your child, and you should trust your own healthy common sense and good instincts.

Last but not least: the following fundamental ethos applies to EMDR as with everything else: please don't go over the top! The idea is to encourage your baby's development, not overstrain it. You will recognise the right amount any time that your baby is content, because s/he feels well. His or her happy smile will thank you. In short: enjoy a wonderful time together.

Limits of self-application

Everything you do should be done in love.
1 Corinthians

Bibliography

[1] See Wissenschaftlicher Beirat Psychotherapie [Scientific Advisory Council Psychotherapy] as per § 11 PsychThG [psychotherapist law] – *Gutachten zur wissenschaftlichen Anerkennung der EMDR-Methode zur Behandlung der Posttraumatischen Belastungsstörung [Survey on the Scientific Recognition of the EMDR Method in the Treatment of Post-Traumatic Stress Disorder]*, in: Dtsch Arztebl 2006; 103(37): A-2417 / B-2098 / C-2022.

[2] See Wikipedia, http://de.wikipedia.org, on EMDR.4

[3] A good overview of studies by T.Hensel (ed.), *EMDR mit Kindern und Jugendlichen [EMDR with Children and Young People]*, Göttingen 2007, pages 15-22.

[4] See A.Madrid/S.Skolek/F.Shapiro, *Repairing Failures in Bonding Through EMDR*, in: CLINICAL CASE STUDIES August 2006, pages 271-286.

[5], [6] See T.Hensel (ed.), *EMDR mit Kindern und Jugendlichen [EMDR with Children and Young People]*, Göttingen 2007, pages 135-141.

[7] See V.Bloemke, *"Es war eine schwere Geburt...": Wie traumatische Erfahrungen verarbeitet werden können ["It was a difficult birth...": Resolving traumatic experiences]*, 3rd edition 2003, pages 144.

[8] See L.Janus/S.Haibach (ed.), *Seelisches Erleben vor und während der Geburt [Spiritual Experiences Before and During Birth]*, 1997, pages 135.

Bibliography

[9] See S.Emge, – *Geburtstrauma – emotionale und psychische Folgen für das Kind in der frühen Kindheit [Birth Trauma: Emotional and Mental Consequences for the Child in Early Childhood]*, examination performance SS 2012, lecturer Fr. Diederichs, Darmstadt Secondary School, page 9; L.Orr/K.Halbig, *Der verbundene Atem, Körper und Seele durch Rebirthing reinigen [Purifying Breath, Body and Soul through Rebirthing]*, 1st edition 2011, pages 103-108.

[10] See F. Renggli, *Der Ursprung der Angst. Antike Mythen und das Trauma der Geburt [The Origin of Fear. Ancient Myths and the Trauma of Birth]*, 2001, page 197.

[11], [12] German Medical Association, *Stellungnahme zur "Aufmerksamkeiysdeficit/Hyperactivitätsstörung (ADHS)" [Attention Deficit/Hyperactivity Disorder (ADHD)]* 26 August 2005, www.bundesaerztekammer.de/downloads/ADHSLang.pdf .

[13] See overview of various research studies by A.Wiater/G. Lehmkuhl, *Handbuch Kinderschlaf: Grundlagen, Diagnostik und Therapie organischer und nichtorganischer Schlafstörungen [Guide to Children's Sleep: Foundations, Diagnostics and Therapy for Organic and Non-Organic Sleep Disorders]*, Stuttgart 2011, pages 164-165.

[14] See footnote [4]

About the author

Ayleen Lyschamaya / Dr. rer. pol. Ayleen Birgit Scheffler-Hadenfeldt was born in Hamburg in 1966. She is a business graduate with a doctorate in international tax law and a non-medical psychotherapy practitioner. She set up her own alternative therapy practice in Berlin where she regularly uses various forms of EMDR in therapy and for holistic spiritual personal development.
https://new-age-enlightenment.com/emdr-trauma-therapy/

In 1988 Ayleen Lyschamaya completed her training as a dance and exercise leader and youth group leader, and since then has taken part regularly in training courses, particularly popular children's sports with an educational component. She has an in the meantime adult son on whom she has also applied the EMDR technique.

Ayleen Lyschamaya provides advice to parents of children who are "different" and/or indigo children, and in some cases supports conventional children's psychotherapies with the use of EMDR. Please visit her website
http://sites.google.com/site/indigokindemdrtherapie

About the author

Competition-free Birthday: Teamwork Games for Kids: Non-competitive Children's Party Games by Ayleen Lyschamaya, new edition 2019.

About the author

Recommended by the youth sports organisation *Württembergische Sportjugend* in the trade magazine *Sport in BW* (2/2010) and in the trade magazine for youth leaders and youth workers *youth and me* (1/2008).

Competitive games are popular at children's birthday parties, often without parents realising the effect these have on the kids. The practical guide *Competition-free Birthday: Teamwork Games for Kids* presents alternatives to traditional games that foster a competitive atmosphere. Instead, *Teamwork Games* strengthen collaboration and cooperation. A clever selection of birthday games can therefore influence the mood of your child's party in a very deliberate fashion.

The advice book *Competition-free Birthday: Teamwork Games for Kids* contains a wide range of merry, exciting, imaginative and fun games for inside and out based on the idea of cooperation and teamwork. It also offers handy hints on how to introduce and develop non-competitive games outside of children's birthday parties. Suggestions on how to link individual games up to create story arcs and themed birthdays go far beyond a simple collection of games to play.

About the author

This guide book will help you create a harmonious birthday celebration thanks to the educational concept of teamwork games plus plenty of practical hints and tips.

Reader reviews:

"… My 5-year-old daughter and her friends had a brilliant time at her birthday party, without any sign of tears or tantrums! Thanks so much!" *Patricia Vogler*, 22.5.2009 on *Amazon*.

"Useful, easy to read, imaginative, highly recommended." *Spielefan*, 16.3.2012 on *Amazon*.

"A fabulous book! The best book on children's parties that I've ever had!" *Sylke Holtz*, 27.2.2013 on *Amazon*.

"… Simply brilliant. We'd buy again." *Steffi from Cologne*, 4.4.2013 on *Amazon*.

"With the help of this book, I was able to organise a really lovely birthday." *Jezirah*, 11.6.2013 on *Amazon*.

https://new-age-enlightenment.com/teamwork-skills/

About the author

Series: *Ayleen Lyschamaya – New Consciousness*

Volume 1: *Spiritual Psychotherapy: the inner family*
   The basic work on the inner family
   The standard work on Spiritual Psychotherapy

Volume 2: *Spiritual EMDR*
   Feelings as a spiritual way to expand one's consciousness

Volume 3: *Completely dissolving feelings of guilt*
   Guilt feelings deletion – live love – approach©
   (Guilt feelings dll-practice©)

Volume 4: *The complete spiritual path*
   The Spiritual Guide Ayleen
   about the Final- Enlightenment
   The basic work on the new spirituality

Volume 5: *Spiritual houseboat holiday in Holland*
   Consciousness shaping with her boyfriend (travelogue)

Volume 6: *Healing the world through
           consciousness development for India*
   Transformation of Buddhism and Hinduism (travelogue)

https://new-age-enlightenment.com/books-spiritual-path/